THE *Life Planning Journal for Women*

THE *Life*
Planning
Journal
for Women

FOR USE WITH

Living Life
on Purpose

Lysa TerKeurst

CONTENTS

Section One

UNDERSTANDING THE FUNDAMENTAL QUESTIONS OF LIFE

Part One

WHAT WILL
A LIFE PLAN
DO FOR ME?

(Refer to Chapter 1 in the *Living Life on Purpose* book)

1. Have you ever stopped to wonder at the amazing way God has created you? Write down ten things wonderful things about yourself. Don't let this be difficult. If you have a hard time, ask God to reveal the things He would have you write down.

2. Write out a prayer of thanksgiving to God for creating you as His special child.

3. God says you are wonderfully made. Journal your thoughts here.

4. Choose three ways that a Life Plan could change your life from those listed in chapter 1 and journal how each could impact you personally.

5. What do you hope to accomplish through this study?

Part Two

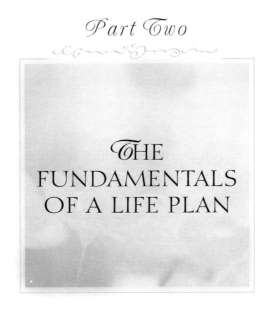

THE FUNDAMENTALS OF A LIFE PLAN

(Refer to Chapter 2 in the *Living Life on Purpose* book)

1. What does it mean to anchor your life to the truth of who God says you are?

2. Draw out a scale as described in chapter 2. Is your scale tipped heavy to the side of what others say about you or heavy on the side of what God says about you?

3. Read Romans 8:31–35 and journal your thoughts about these verses here.

4. Read verse 39 from this same chapter. Can anything separate you from the love of Christ? Journal your thoughts here.

5. How could writing your own fundamental life statements help you?

Part Three

My FOUNDATION

(Refer to chapter 3 in the *Living Life on Purpose* book.)

1. Do you have a personal, growing relationship with Jesus?

2. Is there a void in your life that you have tried to fill with people or things? Explain.

3. Has anything been able to fill you completely? What have you attempted? Explain.

4. Are you relying on God to meet all your needs? Why or why not?

5. Read John 8:32. What does the truth of Jesus need to set you free from?

6. Jeremiah 29:11 says, " 'For I know the plans I have for you,' declares the Lord, 'plans to prosper you and not to harm you, plans to give you hope and a future.' " What promises does God make to you in this verse?

7. According to Hebrews 6:19, the hope found in Jesus serves as an _____ for the soul that is _____ and secure.

8. What foundation is your life built on?

BOOK REVIEW

Now that we know the importance of our foundation being built on our relationship with Jesus, how do we come up with our own foundation statement? Your foundation statement answers the question, "Who are you?" You cannot base this answer on your name, race, job, education, or social status. While all of these are valid descriptions, that is not what we are after here. This "who" question must describe the very essence of your being. Maybe a better way to prompt your answer would be to ask: "Whose are you?" Also, include a sentence or two about your identity and self-worth. To lay the groundwork for each of the statements that will follow your foundation statement, you should simply state that you have a purpose, a mission, a ministry, stages, and principles. End this section with a brief summary of how you view your life. Write your foundation statement here.

Your Foundation Statement:

_____

_____

_____

_____

_____

_____

_____

Part Four

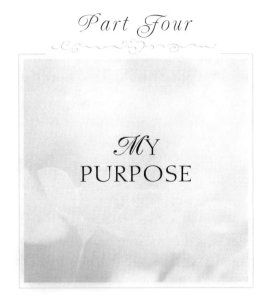

My PURPOSE

(Refer to chapter 4 in the *Living Life on Purpose* book.)

Declare Your Master

1. Romans 12:1: "Therefore, I urge you, brothers, in view of God's mercy, to offer your bodies as living sacrifices, holy and pleasing to God—this is your spiritual act of worship." How do you consider yourself to be a living sacrifice?

2. Are you pursuing holiness? Give examples from your life.

3. How are you seeking to be pleasing to the Lord with your life?

4. Proverbs 3:5 states, "Trust in the Lord with all your heart and lean not on your own understanding." Are you trusting the Lord as this verse instructs?

5. In Luke 16:13, Jesus says, "No servant can serve two masters. Either he will hate the one and love the other, or he will be devoted to the one and despise the other. You cannot serve both God and Money." Are you trying to serve more than one master?

Book Review

Declaring who your master is, is the first step toward defining your purpose. Joshua 24:15 says, "Choose for yourselves this day whom you will serve. . . . But as for me and my household, we will serve the Lord." Joshua commanded the Israelite people to declare their master. To help the people remember that they chose the Lord, he recorded their response and set a stone in place to bear witness to their commitment. We should do the same. Declare your Master by writing it below.

Determine Your Mind-Set

1. Romans 12:2 says, "Do not conform any longer to the pattern of this world, but be transformed by the renewing of your mind. Then you will be able to test and approve what God's will is—his good, pleasing and perfect will." What are some ways you are conforming to the pattern of this world?

2. How can you be transformed?

3. What will be the benefit of renewing your mind?

$\mathcal{B}$OOK REVIEW

You must know what the will of your Master is if you are to do what He has put you here to do. Don't look to the world for your purpose. Look into God's Word. Let your mind be transformed day-by-day. This is part of our purpose—to get alone in silence with our Master and seek His will every day. Don't seek to fill in this part of your purpose with details of tasks to be completed. God will reveal those over time. This part of your purpose statement should be your commitment to seek God with all your mind and make the most of every opportunity He blesses you with. Determine your mind-set by stating what you will allow to be the pattern for your mind. Write it below.

Describe and Develop Your Makeup

1. According to Romans 12:3–6, are you needed by the other members of Christ's body?

2. If you were to describe yourself as a body part, what would you be and why? (An eye? An ear? A leg?)

3. Have you tapped into the rich potential of your God-given gifts? How?

4. According to the Scriptures that mention spiritual gifts (Romans 12:3–6; 1 Corinthians 12:1–11, 27–31; Ephesians 4:11; 1 Peter 4:9–11), what are your spiritual gifts? (If you have never studied spiritual gifts, please refer to Appendix B in *Living Life on Purpose* for an explanation of each gift that may help you better understand your own gifts.)

5. How are you using these gifts?

BOOK REVIEW

We should always remember that our gifts are not given to us so that we can brag about all that we do. They are given so that we can serve others. Our attitude should always be one of thanksgiving that God has chosen, by His grace, to entrust us with such special responsibilities. How are you serving others with your gifts?

Now it is time for you to write your purpose statement. Take some time to ponder your purpose. Remember to declare your Master, determine your mind-set, and describe and develop your makeup. Spend time in prayer and ask God to help you write out a clear and concise purpose statement.

Your Purpose Statement:

_____

_____

_____

_____

_____

_____

_____

_____

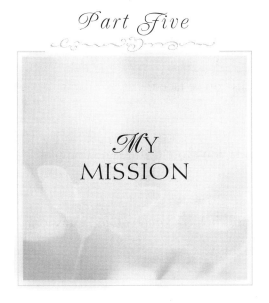

Part Five

My MISSION

(Refer to chapter 5 in the *Living Life on Purpose* book.)

1. Are you willing to do whatever God asks of you?

2. How does the statement "What the devil meant for evil, God can use for good" apply in your life?

3. List the five ways God will equip you for your mission:

   E _____

   Q _____

   U _____

   I _____

   P _____

Experiences

James 1:2–4 says, "Consider it pure joy, my brothers, whenever you face trials of many kinds, because you know that the testing of your faith develops perseverance. Perseverance must finish its work so that you may be mature and complete, not lacking anything."

1. What are some of the trials you've faced?

2. How have these trials made you more mature and complete?

3. How have these experiences helped equip you for a mission?

Qualifications

1. What are some of your skills and abilities?

2. How do your qualifications help equip you for a mission?

Unique Spiritual Gifts

1. Look back at the makeup section of your purpose statement (p. 17). What spiritual gifts did you list there?

2. Do you feel you are seeing your spiritual gifts grow and flourish?
   If yes, how?

   If no, how can you develop them past their seed form?

3. How do your spiritual gifts help equip you for a mission?

Interests

1. What are some of your intense interests?

2. What are some of your fun interests?

3. How do your interests help equip you for a mission?

Personality

1. Are you more of an introverted person or an extroverted person?

2. Are you more of a task-oriented person or a people-oriented person?

3. Do you think God would call you to do something that might challenge your natural personality traits? Why?

4. How does your personality help equip you for your mission?

5. Now that you know what you have been equipped with, list the four major roles you feel called to at this time of your life. For each role write a sentence or two about how you might best utilize what you've been equipped with in each role.

   1) _____

   _____

2) _____
_____

3) _____
_____

4) _____
_____

BOOK REVIEW

God has entrusted us with much. He has given us life, and He wants to see that we are investing our lives wisely. I don't know about you, but I want to make my Master proud. I long to hear, "Well done, My good and faithful servant." To those who give good accounts and live their lives wisely, God will affirm their efforts with encouragement, and He will entrust more to them. Do you want to live an abundant and fulfilling life? Invest your talents wisely. Use what God has given you to fulfill your purpose and answer the call of your mission.

When writing your mission statement include a sentence for each of the major roles that you are currently in. Try to limit these major roles to no more than four.

Write down what you feel God is calling you to do in each of those areas.

Your Mission Statement:

_____
_____
_____
_____
_____
_____
_____
_____
_____

Part Six

My
MINISTRY

(Refer to chapter 6 in the *Living Life on Purpose* book.)

1. Which of the three phases (drifting, determined, or delivered), can you most identify with? Why?

2. What is the key to effective ministry? What does that mean for your own life?

3. Psalm 46:10 says, "Be still, and know that I am God; I will be exalted among the nations, I will be exalted in the earth." When are you still before the Lord?

4. Read Matthew 20:28. Just like Jesus, you are called to your ministry to _____ and not to be _____.

5. What are the three characteristics of a servant?

    1) _____

    2) _____

    3) _____

6. To whom must you submit?

7. Define selflessness. What does this mean for you?

8. What will you have to sacrifice?

9. What rewards are there for serving?

BOOK REVIEW

Now it is time for you to write your own ministry statement. Your statement should clearly state where you are fulfilling your purpose and answering the call of your mission. You should include the place you are serving both where you are needed and where you are gifted. Remember to include a brief description of how you are helping others through your ministry opportunities.

Your Ministry Statement:

_____

_____

_____

_____

_____

_____

_____

_____

_____

_____

Part Seven

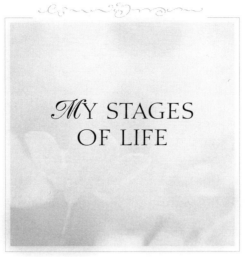

MY STAGES
OF LIFE

(Refer to chapter 7 in the *Living Life on Purpose* book.)

1. Isaiah 61:3 says, "[He has sent me to] provide for those who grieve in Zion—to bestow on them a crown of beauty instead of ashes, the oil of gladness instead of mourning, and a garment of praise instead of a spirit of despair. They will be called oaks of righteousness, a planting of the Lord for the display of his splendor." Why does God give us beauty for ashes, gladness for mourning, and praise for despair?

2. Read Psalm 1:1–3 and John 4:13–14. The psalmist writes, "He will be like a tree firmly planted by streams of water, which yields its fruit in its season, and its leaf does not wither; and in whatever he does, he prospers" (1:3 NASB). According to the verses from Psalm 1 and John 4, where are we to draw our nourishment from?

3. How do the rings of a tree relate to a person's life?

4. What would the rings of your life look like? Take time to draw them here and journal a brief description about each.

5. Which season can you identify with at this time in your life? Why?

6. What opportunities are available to you in this stage of your life?

7. No matter what stage and season of life you are in right now, God _____ _____ you!

8. Why does God want to fill you?

BOOK REVIEW

The stage of life you are in is significant and the spiritual season necessary. Make the most of every blessing you have. Realize that the stumbling blocks you seem to trip over at times may actually be stepping stones leading you closer to God's glory. Vince Lombardi said, "I firmly believe that any man's finest hour—his greatest fulfillment to all he holds dear—is that moment when he has worked his heart out in a good cause and lies exhausted on the field of battle—victorious." No matter what field of battle you are on, work your heart out for God in this stage and season. Your finest hour is coming.

Now it is time for you to write your own stage of life statement. Here are some questions to consider as you do this.

- What roles are you currently playing and what are your responsibilities?
- What is God teaching you through each of the roles that you play?

- What are your time limitations?
- How will you keep your priorities straight?

Your Stage of Life Statement:

_____

_____

_____

_____

_____

_____

_____

_____

_____

_____

Part Eight

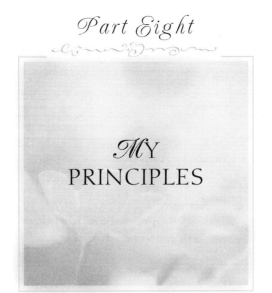

MY PRINCIPLES

(Refer to chapter 8 in the *Living Life on Purpose* book.)

1. Proverbs 31 features a woman who has found the delicate balance between her _____ and her _____.

2. Do you struggle finding this balance sometimes? How?

3. The secret of the Proverbs 31 woman is twofold. First, her strength comes from _____ _____. Second, she has clearly defined her _____ and sets her _____ accordingly.

4. List the Seven Principles of the Proverbs 31 woman:

   (1) _____
   _____

   (2) _____
   _____

   (3) _____
   _____

   (4) _____
   _____

(5) _____

_____

(6) _____

_____

(7) _____

_____

5. Choose three of the characteristics of the Proverbs 31 woman (as described in chapter 8 of the book) that you would like to improve upon in your own life. List them here, and describe how you would like to improve in each area.

(1) _____

_____

_____

_____

(2) _____

_____

_____

_____

(3) _____

_____

_____

_____

Section Two

*LIVING EVERY
AREA OF MY LIFE
ON PURPOSE*

Part Nine

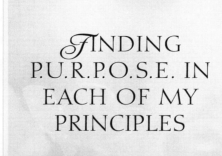

FINDING P.U.R.P.O.S.E. IN EACH OF MY PRINCIPLES

1. Read Acts 5:38–39. Journal your thoughts here.

2. Why is prayer going to be so important as you develop your Life Plan?

3. What does God promise us in Jeremiah 29:11? Journal how this verse encourages you.

4. Read and record Proverbs 16:3 here.

5. What is the world's definition of success?

6. What is God's definition of success?

7. How do we invite God to become intimately involved in our lives?

8. Read and record Romans 12:2 here.

9. How can you know what God's will is?

10. Read Philippians 3:14. Are you dwelling on past failures or are you pressing on as this verse instructs? Journal your thoughts here.

11. What is often the missing link for people in reaching their goals?

12. What qualities should you look for when looking for an accountability partner?

13. Write down the names of a couple of people you would like to start praying about whether God would have one of them be your accountability partner.

Part Ten

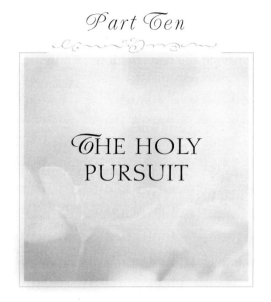

THE HOLY PURSUIT

(Refer to chapter 10 in the *Living Life on Purpose* book.)

PRINCIPLE # 1: The Proverbs 31 woman reveres Jesus Christ as Lord of her life, and pursues an ongoing, personal relationship with Him.

1. Do you struggle at times to pursue an ongoing relationship with Jesus? How?

2. Why do the Scriptures say that the Proverbs 31 woman fears the Lord?

3. Read Isaiah 33:6 and record it here.

4. Where are the joys of life found?

5. Nehemiah 8:10: "Go and enjoy choice food and sweet drinks, and send some to those who have nothing prepared. This day is sacred to our Lord. Do not grieve, for the joy of the Lord is your strength." Where do we draw our strength from?

6. Why should we not try to avoid the construction stops in life?

7. What should we do while waiting on God?

8. Read John 8:12 and record it here.

9. What three divine appointments have had the most monumental effects on your life? Write about them here.

   (1)

   (2)

   (3)

10. What is the key to a successful journey in searching for your purpose as a child of God?

WRITING YOUR LIFE PLAN
(Refer to chapter 9 in the *Living Life on Purpose* book.)

Pray
Take time now to journal specific prayers for yourself as a child of God. Remember to:

   Acknowledge God's sovereign nature and adore His saving grace.

   Confess your sins in this area and ask for forgiveness, remembering always that we must forgive others if we are to be forgiven.

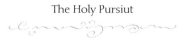

Thank God. List things you are thankful for as a child of God.

Supplication. Ask God for whatever is on your heart. Pray for your specific needs as a child of God.

Here are some suggested scriptural prayers for yourself as a child of God:

- That I might always keep my identity in Christ foremost in my mind and remember that I am a dearly loved child of God (John 1:12; Colossians 3:12; 1 Thessalonians 1:4).

- That I remember I am a daughter of the Most High King and that God is my spiritual Father (Romans 8:14–15).

- That when I struggle, I will always remember that my enemy is not myself, my husband, my children, my friends, or any person. My struggle is against Satan and his evil forces—he is my enemy (Ephesians 6:12).

- That I glorify God by keeping my body pure and healthy because it is the temple of the Holy Spirit who dwells in me (1 Corinthians 6:19–20).

- That the words of my mouth and the meditations of my heart be pleasing to the Lord (Psalm 19:14).

- That I would discipline myself for the purpose of godliness (1 Timothy 4:7).

- That Christ's joy will be in me and that joy made full (John 15:11).

- That I may walk triumphantly with Christ and carry the sweet aroma of the knowledge of Him wherever I go (2 Corinthians 2:14).

_____

_____

_____

_____

_____

_____

_____

_____

_____

_____

_____

_____

_____

_____

_____

Understand God's Word

Journal what God's Word says about your purpose as a child of God and your identity. Review Scriptures we've studied as well as any others you wish to include here.

_____

_____

_____

_____

_____

_____

_____

_____

_____

_____

 Now for a biblical portrait of a woman who knew her purpose as a child of God, let's dig a little deeper into God's Word and study Esther.

The book of Esther starts out with King Xerxes commanding Queen Vashti to appear before him "wearing her royal crown, in order to display her beauty to the people and nobles" Esther 1:11). But she refused to come. A royal decree was put together to ban the queen from the king's presence and to give her royal position to someone else. The search began for a new queen. Esther became that queen.

Disobedience was the reason Queen Vashti was never again to enter the king's presence. First John 5:3 explains why obedience to our Lord is so vital if we are to have an ongoing personal relationship with Him: "This is love for God: to obey his commands. And his commands are not burdensome."

You see, obedience equals love in God's eyes. Write down how you have demonstrated your love to Jesus in this way.

*Q*UESTIONS

1. What made Esther so special to the king? Two things, according to Esther 2:8–16:

• *She prepared herself for her king.*

Before the girl's turn came to go in to King Xerxes, she had to complete twelve months of beauty treatments prescribed for the women; six months with oil of myrrh and six with perfumes and cosmetics. How are you preparing yourself for eternity with Jesus?

- *She pleased the king.*

   Esther 2:4 says, " 'Then let the girl who pleases the king be queen instead of Vashti.' This advice appealed to the king, and he followed it." What does this verse say the king was looking for the queen to do?

2. "Now the king was attracted to Esther more than to any of the other women, and she won his favor and approval more than any of the other virgins. So he set a royal crown on her head and made her queen instead of Vashti" (Esther 2:17). How are you pleasing Jesus today? How have you touched the heart of Jesus today?

3. Esther was placed in a position of royalty by the mighty hand of God. His people needed help and Esther was in a position for God to use her. Maybe you, too, have come to your royal position in Christ for such a time as this (Esther 4:14b). Record your thoughts here.

4. Esther was an obedient vessel for God to use for His glory. She was willing to be obedient to her call even to the point of giving up her life. "If I perish, I perish" (Esther 4:16). What might you have to give up in order to be obedient to your call?

5. The king wanted to grant Esther any request she asked. She went before him and asked for favor. "If I have found favor with you, O king, and if it pleases your majesty, grant me my life—this is my petition. And spare my people—this is my request" (Esther 7:3).

   Who would you like to lift before the throne today? He wants to grant your request. Is it the salvation of a loved one? Is it a broken heart that needs mending? Is it a miracle? Your miracle is on its way! You have found favor with the King of kings! Journal your answer here.

_____

_____

_____

_____

_____

Record Key Scriptures

Journal Scriptures here where God has revealed a spiritual truth to you. Write the verse and what you feel God wants you to understand through His Word. Remember, each time you experience a spiritual marker in your role as a child of God, pull this section of your Life Plan out and write it down. If you run out of room in this journal, continue your writings on separate paper and keep them in a special notebook.

_____

_____

_____

_____

_____

_____

_____

_____

_____

_____

_____

_____

_____

_____

Plan Your Goals

Write down your goals for yourself as a child of God.

_____

_____

_____

_____

_____

Outline Your Action Steps

List your goals from above here, and under each one write out the necessary action steps needed to help you reach it.

Goal: _____

Action Steps: (1)_____ Deadline:_____

(2)_____ Deadline:_____
(3)_____ Deadline:_____
(4)_____ Deadline:_____

Goal: _____

Action Steps: (1)_____ Deadline:_____
(2)_____ Deadline:_____
(3)_____ Deadline:_____
(4)_____ Deadline:_____

Goal: _____

Action Steps: (1)_____ Deadline:_____
(2)_____ Deadline:_____
(3)_____ Deadline:_____
(4)_____ Deadline:_____

Goal: _____

Action Steps: (1)_____ Deadline:_____
(2)_____ Deadline:_____
(3)_____ Deadline:_____
(4)_____ Deadline:_____

Goal: _____

Action Steps: (1)_____ Deadline:_____
(2)_____ Deadline:_____
(3)_____ Deadline:_____
(4)_____ Deadline:_____

Set a Realistic Schedule

Decide on a realistic deadline to accomplish each of your action steps. Make sure you write them above and on your calendar. If an action step is ongoing, such as having quiet time with the Lord, write "daily" beside it, and remember to schedule time for it each day.

Examine Your Progress

Write a plan here to examine your progress. If you plan to meet with an accountability partner or group, write out specific questions they should ask you. List areas in your relationship with the Lord they should ask you about and how they can pray for you. Specific questions and prayer requests:

_____

_____

_____

_____

_____

Here are some questions to consider from chapter 9 of *Living Life on Purpose*:

- Am I glorifying God in this area of my life?

- Am I working toward fulfilling my purpose in this area? How?

- How is my prayer life? Am I regularly praying for this area of my life?

- What have I recently learned from God's Word about this area of my life?

- What Scripture have I memorized to help me in this area?

- What action steps have I completed to help me move closer toward meeting some of my goals for this area?

- What goal or goals have I met?

- Am I managing my schedule well? Am I putting the "rocks" of my life first? Are there activities I need to eliminate from my schedule?

- Whom do I have to hold me accountable in this area of my life?

- Am I seeing positive life changes from having a Life Plan? If yes, list some of those here. If no, write out why not.

You will notice that that there is enough room in your journal to examine your progress as a child of God once a month for one year.

JANUARY

_____
_____
_____
_____

FEBRUARY

_____
_____
_____
_____

MARCH

_____
_____
_____
_____

APRIL

_____
_____
_____
_____

MAY

_____
_____
_____
_____

JUNE

_____
_____
_____

JULY

_____

_____

_____

_____

AUGUST

_____

_____

_____

_____

SEPTEMBER

_____

_____

_____

_____

OCTOBER

_____

_____

_____

_____

NOVEMBER

_____

_____

_____

_____

DECEMBER

_____

_____

_____

Part Eleven

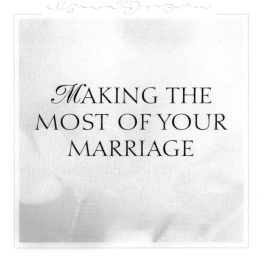

MAKING THE MOST OF YOUR MARRIAGE

(Refer to chapter 11 in the *Living Life on Purpose* book.)

PRINCIPLE # 2: The Proverbs 31 woman loves, honors, and respects her husband as head of the home.

1. Paul writes in Ephesians 5:22 and 33, "Wives, submit to your husbands as to the Lord. . . . and the wife must respect her husband." What does God expect from you as a wife?

2. What does Proverbs 19:13 warn us not to be? Have you sprung any leaks lately?

3. Who is able to shape and mold you into the wife your husband needs?

4. Paul writes in Philippians 1:6, "He who began a good work in you will carry it on to completion until the day of Christ Jesus." Who will carry out His good work in you?

5. In Genesis 2:18 the Lord says, "It is not good for the man to be alone. I will make a helper suitable for him." Have you caught yourself being more of a "complainer" than a "completer"? What are some ways you can be a suitable helper for your husband?

6. Read 1 Corinthians 13:4–8. List the characteristics of love as described in this passage. Put a star by the ones you do well and circle the ones you need to work on.

_____

_____

_____

_____

_____

_____

7. Write a commitment to pursue God's definition of love in your marriage.

8. List the five greatest needs of a man. Under each one write two things you could do to better meet his needs. (You can use the list of creative ideas from the *Living Life on Purpose* book or make up your own.)

  (1) _____

    ★ _____

    ★ _____

  (2) _____

    ★ _____

    ★ _____

  (3) _____

    ★ _____

    ★ _____

  (4) _____

    ★ _____

    ★ _____

(5) _____

★ _____

★ _____

9. Now write those special "to dos" in your calendar. Put a check mark here when you have scheduled them. ❏

WRITING YOUR LIFE PLAN

(Refer to chapter 9 in the *Living Life on Purpose* book.)

Pray

Take time now to journal specific prayers for yourself as a wife. Remember to:

Acknowledge that only God can meet your every need, and adore Him for being willing and able to do so.

Confess your sins in this area and ask for forgiveness, remembering always that we must forgive others if we are to be forgiven.

Thank God. Write out your prayers of thanksgiving. List things you are thankful for as a wife.

Supplication. Ask God for whatever is on your heart. Pray for your specific needs as a wife. Also, write out specific prayers for your husband.

Here are some suggested scriptural prayers for yourself as a wife:
- That my expectations for my marriage come only from God (Psalm 62:5).
- That I submit to my husband's leadership in my home (Ephesians 5:22, 24).
- That I respect my husband (Ephesians 5:33).
- That my attitude toward my husband always be centered in godly actions and not hurtful words (1 Peter 3:1–2).
- That I would not be quarrelsome and ill-tempered (Proverbs 21:19).
- That I love my husband the way he needs to be loved (Titus 2:4).

Here are some suggested scriptural prayers for you to pray for your husband:
- That Christ may dwell in his heart through faith and that his life would be rooted and grounded in Christ's love (Ephesians 3:17).
- That he love you, his wife, as you need to be loved (Ephesians 5:33).

- That he rely on Christ to do abundantly beyond all he asks or thinks, according to Christ's power in him (Ephesians 3:20).
- That the Lord would establish the work of his hands (Psalm 90:17).
- That he would be neither a workaholic nor lazy. That he would keep his work in balance and enjoy the good of his labor as a gift from God (Proverbs 13:4; 21:25; Ecclesiastes 3:13).
- That he would not grow weary in doing good, for in due season he will reap a reward if he does not lose heart (Galatians 6:9).
- That he would walk not in the flesh but according to the Spirit. That the fruits of the Spirit would become more and more evident in his life (Galatians 5:22–23).
- That he would take on the full armor of God and be able to stand firm against the schemes of Satan (Ephesians 6:10–18).
- That he would not be deceived by the lusts and sins of the world. That he would put aside all filthiness and all wickedness and in humility receive the word of God. Then may he be a doer of the Word and not merely a hearer only (James 1:14–16; 21–23).
- That he would be a good father who correctly disciplines, wisely trains, and gently loves his children (Proverbs 3:12; 23:24; 29:17).
- That he would call on the name of the Lord to be his deliverer, his strength, the one in whom he trusts, his shield, and his salvation (Psalm 18:2–3).
- That God would perfect, confirm, strengthen, and establish him to be the man He created him to be (1 Peter 5:10–11).

_____

_____

_____

_____

_____

_____

_____

_____

_____

_____

_____

_____

Understand God's Word

Journal what God's Word says about your purpose as a wife. Review Scriptures we've studied as well as any others you wish to include here.

_____

_____

_____

_____

_____

_____

_____

_____

_____

_____

 Now for a biblical portrait of a woman who knew her purpose as a wife, let's dig a little deeper into God's Word and study Rebekah.

I love the story in Genesis 24 of Rebekah and Isaac. Isaac's father, Abraham, sent his most trusted servant, Eliezer (15:2–3) out to look for a bride for his beloved son.

QUESTIONS

1. Whom did Eliezer ask to help him with this difficult task? (Genesis 24:12–14)

2. Do you have a difficult situation going on in your home that you want to bring to God?

3. According to Genesis 24:15, when did God answer Eliezer's prayer?

4. When Rebekah came on the scene, Eliezer hurried over to her. Genesis 24:17–20: "The servant hurried to meet her and said, 'Please give me a little water from your jar.' . . . After she had given him a drink, she said, 'I'll draw water for your camels too, until they have finished drinking.' So she quickly emptied her jar into the trough, ran back to the well to draw more water, and drew enough for all his camels." Eliezer is watching a kind, considerate, compassionate servant at work. What would he find you doing today for the leader of your home?

5. Now let's read one more verse and find out whether or not Eliezer's trip was successful. "Without saying a word, the man watched her closely to learn whether or not the LORD had made his journey successful" (Genesis 24:21). If someone were watching you closely without your knowing about it, would he or she find a wife of character? One that honors, loves, and respects?

6. What qualities of Christ are you portraying to your husband? How can you improve?

7. Eliezer described Rebekah when he saw her. "The girl was very beautiful, a virgin; no man had ever lain with her. She went down to the spring, filled her jar and came up again" (Genesis 24:16). How would your husband describe you?

8. Now read how Rebekah described herself. "She answered him, 'I am the daughter of Bethuel, the son that Milcah bore to Nahor.' And she added, 'We have plenty of straw and fodder, as well as room for you to spend the night'" (Genesis 24:24–25). She answered his question out of respect and then immediately thought of his well-being. Thinking of others first is the key to a successful marriage, or any relationship for that matter. Isn't she an amazing woman? Remember, this man is looking for a perfect bride for his master's son. Isaac was heir to the family fortune and business. Eliezer must have been very impressed with her unselfish, warm, caring nature. God certainly does answer prayers, doesn't He? What prayer do you have for your mate today?

9. What characteristic of Christ are you praying for in your husband? If you aren't praying for him, who is?

10. Last, notice that neither Eliezer nor Rebekah's family ever forced her to go with him. "Then they said, 'Let's call the girl and ask her about it.' So they called Rebekah and asked her, 'Will you go with this man?' 'I will go,' she said" (Genesis 24:57–58). What is your choice today? Will you love this man? Will you honor this man? Will you respect this man? Will you pray for this man? Will you believe in this man? God hopes so. Write your commitment here.

Record Key Scriptures

Journal Scriptures here where God reveals a spiritual truth to you. Write the verse and what you feel God wants you to understand through His Word. Remember, each time you experience a spiritual marker in your role as a wife, pull this section of your Life Plan out and write it down. If you run out of room in this journal, continue your writings on separate paper and keep them in a special notebook.

_____
_____
_____
_____
_____
_____
_____
_____
_____
_____

Plan Your Goals

Write down your goals for yourself as a wife.

_____
_____
_____
_____
_____

Outline Your Action Steps

List your goals from above here, and under each one write out the necessary action steps needed to help you reach those goals.

Goal: _____

Action Steps: (1)_____ Deadline:_____
      (2)_____ Deadline:_____
      (3)_____ Deadline:_____
      (4)_____ Deadline:_____

Goal: _____

Action Steps: (1)_____ Deadline:_____
      (2)_____ Deadline:_____
      (3)_____ Deadline:_____
      (4)_____ Deadline:_____

Goal: _____

Action Steps: (1)_____ Deadline:_____

            (2)_____ Deadline:_____

            (3)_____ Deadline:_____

            (4)_____ Deadline:_____

Goal: _____

Action Steps: (1)_____ Deadline:_____

            (2)_____ Deadline:_____

            (3)_____ Deadline:_____

            (4)_____ Deadline:_____

Goal: _____

Action Steps: (1)_____ Deadline:_____

            (2)_____ Deadline:_____

            (3)_____ Deadline:_____

            (4)_____ Deadline:_____

Set a Realistic Schedule

Decide on a realistic deadline to accomplish each of your action steps. Make sure you schedule those steps above and on your calendar. If an action step is ongoing, write "daily" beside it and remember to schedule time for it each day.

Examine Your Progress

Write a plan here to examine your progress. If you plan to meet with an accountability partner or group, write out specific questions they should ask you. List areas in your relationship with your husband they should ask you about and how they can pray for you.

Specific questions and prayer requests:

_____

_____

_____

_____

_____

Here are some questions to consider from chapter 9 of *Living Life on Purpose*:

- Am I glorifying God in this area of my life?

- Am I working toward fulfilling my purpose in this area? How?

- How is my prayer life? Am I regularly praying for this area of my life?

- What have I recently learned from God's Word about this area of my life?

- What Scripture have I memorized to help me in this area?

- What action steps have I completed to help me move closer toward meeting some of my goals for this area?

- What goal or goals have I met?

- Am I managing my schedule well? Am I putting the "rocks" of my life first? Are there activities I need to eliminate from my schedule?

- Whom do I have to hold me accountable in this area of my life?

- Am I seeing positive life changes from having a Life Plan? If yes, list some of those here. If no, write out why not.

You will notice that there is enough room in your journal to examine your progress as a wife once a month for one year.

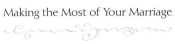

JANUARY

_____

_____

_____

_____

FEBRUARY

_____

_____

_____

_____

MARCH

_____

_____

_____

_____

APRIL

_____

_____

_____

_____

MAY

_____

_____

_____

JUNE

_____

_____

_____

JULY

_____
_____
_____
_____

AUGUST

_____
_____
_____
_____

SEPTEMBER

_____
_____
_____
_____

OCTOBER

_____
_____
_____
_____

NOVEMBER

_____
_____
_____
_____

DECEMBER

_____
_____
_____

Part Twelve

THE HIGH CALLING OF MOTHERHOOD

(Refer to chapter 12 in the *Living Life on Purpose* book.)

PRINCIPLE # 3: The Proverbs 31 woman nurtures her children and believes that motherhood is a high calling with the responsibility of shaping and molding the children who will one day define who we are as a community and nation.

1. In Isaiah 49:16 God says, "See, I have engraved you on the palms of my hands." Do you trust God to hold on to your children?

2. Journal a prayer here entrusting your children to God.

3. Do you ever catch yourself losing your joy in this adventure known as motherhood?

4. Has God ever given you an experience that helped you keep things in perspective as a mom? Journal that experience here.

5. Have you ever caught yourself wishing away your children's childhood?

6. Journal your thoughts after reading the poem "The Writing on the Wall" from chapter 12 of *Living Life on Purpose.*

7. List some ways you are helping shape the eternally significant lives of your children.

8. Read Joshua 1:6–9. Journal how God speaks to your heart through these verses.

9. Read over "The Pleasing Principles" in chapter 12 of *Living Life on Purpose* and list some that you are doing well.

10. Now write down some principles you need to work on.

11. If you desire to write a blessing for your children, take time to work on it now. Once you complete it, write it here:

12. What is the greatest way for you to guard and protect your children?

13. What is the greatest wisdom you can share?

14. What is the best example you can set?

15. What is the greatest gift you can pass on?

Writing Your Life Plan

(Refer to chapter 9 in the *Living Life on Purpose* book.)

Pray

Take time now to journal specific prayers for yourself as a mother. Remember to:

Acknowledge God as the Divine Creator, and adore Him for the miracle of life.

Confess your sins in this area and ask for forgiveness, remembering always that we must forgive others if we are to be forgiven.

Thank God. Write out your prayers of thanksgiving. List things you are thankful for as a mother.

Supplication. Ask God for whatever is on your heart. Pray for your specific needs as a mother. Also, write out specific prayers for your children.

Here are some suggested scriptural prayers for you as a mother:

- That I will leave behind any sins or generational strongholds passed down to me from previous generations because I am a new creation in Christ. The old has gone, the new has come! Teach me to be the mother you want me to be (2 Corinthians 5:17).
- That God will instruct and teach me in the way I should go as a mother. God, please counsel me and watch over my family and me (Psalm 32:8).
- That I will cast all my anxiety on Him because He cares for my children and me (1 Peter 5:7).
- That my walk will be blameless and worthy to be followed. That God will be my shield (Psalm 84:11).
- That I would not embitter or discourage my children, but instead bring them up in the training and instruction of the Lord (Ephesians 6:4; Colossians 3:21).
- That I would have only good things stored up in my heart so that when I speak, the overflow of my heart will be good for my children to hear (Luke 6:45).

Here are some suggested scriptural prayers to pray for your children:

- That early in life they would accept Jesus Christ as Lord of their life and know what it means to be born again of the spirit. That they would come to a full knowledge of the truth that sets them free (Psalm 71:5; John 3:3–7; 8:32; 1 Timothy 2:3–4).
- That they would be physically, emotionally, and spiritually healthy (Exodus 23:25; Isaiah 53:5; Jeremiah 30:17).
- That they would be quick to listen, slow to speak, and slow to become angry. That they would live the righteous life that God desires (Psalm 37:8; James 1:19–20).
- That they would be obedient to the godly training of their parents. That they would be protected from choosing the wrong kinds of friends. That they would not be enticed by the sins of the world but rather be pure and right in their conduct (Proverbs 1:10; 6:20; 20:11).
- That they would be strong and courageous. That they would stand firm in their faith and learn to love God's Word. That they would not be afraid because the Lord our God is with them wherever they go (Joshua 1:8–9; 2 Kings 6:16; Isaiah 40:29; 1 Corinthians 16:13).
- That they and the one they are to marry would flee the evil desires of youth. That they would be kept pure for marriage. That they would pursue righteousness, faith, love, and peace. That they would be surrounded by people who call on the Lord out of pure hearts (2 Timothy 2:22; Hebrews 13:4).
- That they learn to hear God's voice leading them in His paths. That they take to heart His counsel and bring great joy to the Lord as they walk in His truth (Isaiah 2:3; 30:21).

_____

_____

_____

_____

_____

_____

_____

_____

_____

_____

_____

_____

Understand God's Word

Journal what God's Word says about your purpose as a mother. Review Scriptures we've studied as well as any others you wish to include here.

_____

_____

_____

_____

_____

_____

_____

_____

_____

_____

_____

_____

 Now, for a biblical portrait of a woman who knew her purpose as a mother, let's dig a little deeper into God's Word and study Hannah.

For reasons only a sovereign God knows, Hannah was barren. "The LORD closed her womb" (1 Samuel 1:5). In bitterness of soul Hannah wept much, and she prayed to the Lord for a son (v. 10). Scripture tells us that she kept praying and would not give up.

Have you ever prayed and prayed to God on behalf of your child? Have you ever prayed and prayed and prayed for a prodigal child to come home? Have you ever prayed earnestly for your child's health or salvation? The story of Hannah should ground you in hope.

Read how the Lord answered Hannah's prayer in 1 Samuel 1:19b–20. "Elkanah lay with Hannah his wife, and the Lord remembered her. So in the course of time Hannah conceived and gave birth to a son. She named him Samuel, saying, 'Because I asked the Lord for him.'"

Never ever give up praying for a child or for your children. I want you to notice a very important phrase in the above Scripture: "So in the course of time . . ." All of your prayers are "remembered" by the Lord and answered in His timing and in His will. He wants to grant you the desires of your heart (Psalm 37:4). It is God's will for our children to prosper. We just have to trust in the sovereignty of God.

However, there is a key Scripture to remember. First Samuel 1:28 says, "So now I give him to the LORD. For his whole life he will be given over to the LORD."

QUESTIONS

1. Have you trusted the Lord with the lives of your little ones?

2. Are you teaching them daily to walk with their heavenly Father? How?

3. Do you feed them from the Word of God on a regular basis?

"Train a child in the way he should go, and when he is old he will not turn from it" (Proverbs 22:6). We must understand that this verse is a promise from God. The key is to trust their days, minutes, and hours to their heavenly Father, their Creator.

Hannah understood the sovereignty of God. I want you to read her prayer to God after she gave Samuel back to Him. Is this the God you know?

HANNAH'S PRAYER
(1 Samuel 2:1–10)

"My heart rejoices in the LORD;
in the LORD my horn is lifted high.
My mouth boasts over my enemies,
for I delight in your deliverance.

"There is no one holy like the LORD;
there is no one besides you;
there is no Rock like our God.

"Do not keep talking so proudly
or let your mouth speak such arrogance,
for the LORD is a God who knows,

and by him deeds are weighed.
"The bows of the warriors are broken,
but those who stumbled are armed with strength.
Those who were full hire themselves out for food,
but those who were hungry hunger no more.
She who was barren has borne seven children,
but she who has had many sons pines away.

"The LORD brings death and makes alive;
he brings down to the grave and raises up.
The LORD sends poverty and wealth;
he humbles and he exalts.
He raises the poor from the dust
and lifts the needy from the ash heap;
he seats them with princes
and has them inherit a throne of honor.

"For the foundations of the earth are
the LORD's; upon them he has set the world.
He will guard the feet of his saints,
but the wicked will be silenced in darkness.

"It is not by strength that one prevails;
those who oppose the LORD will be shattered.
He will thunder against them from heaven;
the LORD will judge the ends of the earth.

"He will give strength to his king and exalt
the horn of his anointed."

Motherhood is a very high calling. God entrusted Jesus to Mary. God entrusted Samuel to Hannah. Now He is entrusting His little ones to you! Your little one could be a person who changes the whole world. Dream big for your children and go boldly to the throne for them. You may be asking yourself, "How do I do that?" Well, Hannah would say, "Just ask Him!" Journal a prayer here.

Record Key Scriptures

Journal Scriptures here where God reveals a spiritual truth to you. Write the verse and what you feel God wants you to understand through His Word. Remember, each time you experience a spiritual marker in your role as a mother, pull this section of your Life Plan out and write it down. If you run out of room in this journal, continue your writings on separate paper and keep them in a special notebook.

_____

_____

_____

_____

_____

_____

_____

_____

_____

_____

Plan Your Goals

Write down goals for yourself as a mother.

_____

_____

_____

_____

Outline Your Action Steps

List your goals from above here, and under each one write out the necessary action steps needed to help you reach your goals.

Goal: _____

Action Steps: (1)_____ Deadline:_____

(2)_____ Deadline:_____

(3)_____ Deadline:_____

(4)_____ Deadline:_____

Goal: _____

Action Steps: (1)_____ Deadline:_____
              (2)_____ Deadline:_____
              (3)_____ Deadline:_____
              (4)_____ Deadline:_____

Goal: _____

Action Steps: (1)_____ Deadline:_____
              (2)_____ Deadline:_____
              (3)_____ Deadline:_____
              (4)_____ Deadline:_____

Goal: _____

Action Steps: (1)_____ Deadline:_____
              (2)_____ Deadline:_____
              (3)_____ Deadline:_____
              (4)_____ Deadline:_____

Goal: _____

Action Steps: (1)_____ Deadline:_____
              (2)_____ Deadline:_____
              (3)_____ Deadline:_____
              (4)_____ Deadline:_____

Set a Realistic Schedule

Decide on a realistic deadline to accomplish each of your action steps. Make sure you schedule those steps above and on your calendar. If an action step is ongoing, write "daily" beside it, and remember to schedule time for it each day.

Examine Your Progress

Write a plan here to examine your progress. If you plan to meet with an accountability partner or group, write out specific questions they should ask you. List areas in your role as a mother they should ask you about and how they can pray for you. Specific questions and prayer requests:

_____

_____

_____

_____

Here are some questions to consider from chapter 9 of *Living Life on Purpose:*

- Am I glorifying God in this area of my life?

- Am I working toward fulfilling my purpose in this area? How?

- How is my prayer life? Am I regularly praying for this area of my life?

- What have I recently learned from God's Word about this area of my life?

- What Scripture have I memorized to help me in this area?

- What action steps have I completed to help me move closer toward meeting some of my goals for this area?

- What goal or goals have I met?

- Am I managing my schedule well? Am I putting the "rocks" of my life first? Are there activities I need to eliminate from my schedule?

- Whom do I have to hold me accountable in this area of my life?

- Am I seeing positive life changes from having a Life Plan? If yes, list some of those here. If no, write out why not.

You will notice that there is enough room in your journal to examine your progress as a mother once a month for one year.

JANUARY

_____

_____

_____

_____

FEBRUARY

_____

_____

_____

_____

MARCH

_____

_____

_____

_____

APRIL

_____

_____

_____

_____

MAY

_____

_____

_____

_____

JUNE

_____

_____

_____

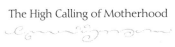

JULY

_____
_____
_____
_____

AUGUST

_____
_____
_____
_____

SEPTEMBER

_____
_____
_____
_____

OCTOBER

_____
_____
_____
_____

NOVEMBER

_____
_____
_____
_____

DECEMBER

_____
_____
_____
_____

Part Thirteen

THERE'S NO PLACE LIKE HOME

(Refer to chapter 13 in the *Living Life on Purpose* book.)

PRINCIPLE # 4: The Proverbs 31 woman is a disciplined and industrious keeper of the home who creates a warm and loving environment for her family and friends.

1. Is it evident that God's love fills your home? Why or why not?

2. Proverbs 24:3 says, "By wisdom a house is built, and through understanding it is established; through knowledge its rooms are filled with rare and beautiful treasures." Besides material possessions, what rare and beautiful treasures fill your home?

3. What would your family say are their favorite parts of your home?

4. Read Proverbs 31:27. How do you watch over the affairs of your household?

5. Do you have a plan for keeping your home clean and in order?

6. Ask each member of your family what their definition of a "haven" is. Record their responses here.

7. How do you keep your arms strong for your tasks?

8. What are some creative ways you could fit exercising into your schedule?

9. Do you consider it a privilege to be the keeper of your home?

10. Journal what you are most thankful for here.

WRITING YOUR LIFE PLAN
(Refer to chapter 9 in the *Living Life on Purpose* book.)

Pray

Take time now to journal specific prayers for yourself as a keeper of the home. Remember to:

Acknowledge God as our divine comforter, and adore Him for creating our eternal homes.

Confess your sins in this area and ask for forgiveness, remembering always that we must forgive others if we are to be forgiven.

Thank God. Write out prayers of thanksgiving. List things you are thankful for as a keeper of the home.

Supplication. Ask God for whatever is on your heart. Pray for your specific needs as a keeper of the home. Also, write out specific prayers for your home.

Here are some suggested scriptural prayers for your home:

- That all those in my home and I will choose to serve the Lord (Joshua 24:15).

- That my home be a place where my children learn about the Lord both in words and the actions they see modeled here. That my husband and I talk about the Lord and be faithful to pray as a family at all times (Deuteronomy 11:19; Psalm 78:4–7).

- That I would be a faithful keeper of the home and watch over the affairs of my household (Proverbs 31:27; Titus 2:5).

- That I would build my home on the wisdom of the Lord. That I would establish my home through understanding, and that I would fill it with the rare and beautiful treasures of the knowledge of the Lord (Proverbs 24:3–4).

- That my home be a reflection of God's love. That all who enter through our door be touched by the Scriptures we have displayed throughout our home and by seeing His Word lived out (Deuteronomy 6:8–9).

_____

_____

_____

_____

_____

_____

_____

_____

_____

_____

_____

_____

_____

_____

_____

_____

_____

_____

Understand God's Word

Journal what God's Word says about your purpose as a keeper of the home. Review Scriptures we've studied as well as any others you wish to include here.

_____

_____

_____

_____

_____

_____

_____

_____

_____

Now for a biblical portrait of a woman who knew her purpose as a keeper of the home, let's dig a little deeper into God's Word and study the widow at Zarephath.

The saying "home is where the heart is" is simple but so true. Let's give a little more personality to that familiar phrase. Someone has described a home as "a place or environment natural or dear to one because of personal relationships or feelings of comfort and security. A peaceful or restful place; refuge; haven."

QUESTIONS

1. Is your home a place that is dear to you? Why or why not?

2. Is your home a place of comfort and security? Why or why not?

3. Is your home a peaceful, restful refuge? Why or why not?

4. What makes your home a haven for those you love?

Ask yourself, what could I do today in my home to assure my husband's happiness and comfort? What would tickle the hearts of my children today? Is it a hot meal, clean house, or

the smell of fresh baked cookies? Maybe your husband enjoys color-coordinated sock draw-
ers. Maybe he likes his shirts pressed a certain way. Maybe it is having enough time to play
Clue or Operation with your children. Maybe it's making pillow and blanket forts all over
the family room. Only you can figure out what brightens your loved ones' faces. Write some
things you can think of to create pleasure in your home for each member of your family.

Next step . . . do it! Pull out your schedule and write those ideas in it. Put a check mark
in this box when you've scheduled them. ❏

Let's look at a woman who did it! She is referred to as the widow at Zarephath. God was
using Elijah the prophet in a mighty way (1 Kings 17). The Lord sent Elijah to a place called
Zarephath of Sidon. He was instructed to "go at once" (v. 9). There the Lord had commanded a widow to supply Elijah with food.

First Kings 17:10 records what happened: "So he went to Zarephath. When he came to
the town gate, a widow was there gathering sticks. He called to her and asked, 'Would you
bring me a little water in a jar so I may have a drink?' As she was going to get it, he called,
'And bring me, please, a piece of bread.' "

The story goes on that the woman was distressed because she didn't have any bread. She
only had a handful of flour in a jar and a little oil in a jug. She was anticipating that she and
her son were to die of starvation. Elijah told her not to be afraid and to go home and pre-
pare a meal. " 'The jar of flour will not be used up and the jug of oil will not run dry until
the day the LORD gives rain on the land.' She went away and did as Elijah had told her. So
there was food every day for Elijah and for the woman and her family. For the jar of flour
was not used up and the jug of oil did not run dry, in keeping with the word of the LORD
spoken by Elijah" (1 Kings 17:14–16).

5. Is your home run on the skimpiness of this world, or is it flourishing on the provision of
   God?

6. What areas of your home life can you turn over to the power of God?

7. The story doesn't end there. God used Elijah to perform a miracle in the widow's home.
   What miracle do you need today?

8. First Kings tells us that Elijah was in the widow's home a pretty long time. I believe that Elijah had a hard time leaving her. Is your home full of the provisions of God? Do you create such a warm, and loving atmosphere in your home that people don't want to leave? If God dwells in your home, you can change the old saying "Home is where the heart is" into, "My home is where God's heart is!" Journal your thoughts here.

_____
_____
_____
_____
_____
_____
_____

Record Key Scriptures

Journal Scriptures here where God reveals a spiritual truth to you. Write the verse and what you feel God wants you to understand through His Word. Remember, each time you experience a spiritual marker in your role as a keeper of the home, pull this section of your Life Plan out and write it down. If you run out of room in this journal, continue your writings on separate paper and keep them in a special notebook.

_____
_____
_____
_____
_____
_____
_____

Plan Your Goals

Write down your goals for yourself as a keeper of the home.

_____
_____
_____
_____
_____

Outline Your Action Steps

List your goals from above here, and under each one write out the necessary action steps needed to help you reach it.

Goal: _____

Action Steps: (1)_____ Deadline:_____

(2)_____ Deadline:_____

(3)_____ Deadline:_____

(4)_____ Deadline:_____

Goal: _____

Action Steps: (1)_____ Deadline:_____

(2)_____ Deadline:_____

(3)_____ Deadline:_____

(4)_____ Deadline:_____

Goal: _____

Action Steps: (1)_____ Deadline:_____

(2)_____ Deadline:_____

(3)_____ Deadline:_____

(4)_____ Deadline:_____

Goal: _____

Action Steps: (1)_____ Deadline:_____

(2)_____ Deadline:_____

(3)_____ Deadline:_____

(4)_____ Deadline:_____

Goal: _____

Action Steps: (1)_____ Deadline:_____

(2)_____ Deadline:_____

(3)_____ Deadline:_____

(4)_____ Deadline:_____

Set a Realistic Schedule

Decide on a realistic deadline to accomplish each of your action steps. Make sure you schedule those steps above and on your calendar. If an action step is ongoing, write "daily" beside it and remember to schedule time for it each day.

Examine Your Progress

Write a plan to examine your progress here. If you plan to meet with an accountability partner or group, write out specific questions they should ask you. List areas in your role as a keeper of the home they should ask you about and how they can pray for you. Specific questions and prayer requests:

_____

_____

_____

_____

_____

Here are some questions to consider from chapter 9 of *Living Life on Purpose:*

- Am I glorifying God in this area of my life?

- Am I working toward fulfilling my purpose in this area? How?

- How is my prayer life? Am I regularly praying for this area of my life?

- What have I recently learned from God's Word about this area of my life?

- What Scripture have I memorized to help me in this area?

- What action steps have I completed to help me move closer toward meeting some of my goals for this area?

- What goal or goals have I met?

- Am I managing my schedule well? Am I putting the "rocks" of my life first? Are there activities I need to eliminate from my schedule?

- Whom do I have to hold me accountable in this area of my life?

- Am I seeing positive life changes from having a Life Plan? If yes, list some of those here. If no, write out why not.

You will notice that there is enough room in your journal to examine your progress as a keeper of the home once a month for one year.

JANUARY

_____

_____

_____

_____

FEBRUARY

_____

_____

_____

_____

MARCH

_____

_____

_____

_____

APRIL

_____

_____

_____

_____

MAY

_____

_____

_____

_____

JUNE

_____

_____

_____

JULY

_____

_____

_____

_____

AUGUST

_____

_____

_____

_____

SEPTEMBER

_____

_____

_____

_____

OCTOBER

_____

_____

_____

_____

NOVEMBER

_____

_____

_____

_____

DECEMBER

_____

_____

_____

Part Fourteen

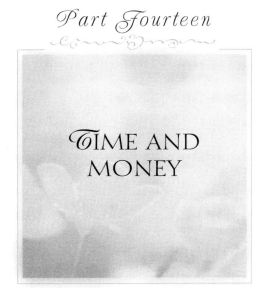

TIME AND
MONEY

(Refer to chapter 14 in the *Living Life on Purpose* book.)

PRINCIPLE # 5: The Proverbs 31 woman contributes to the financial well-being of her household by being a faithful steward of the time and money God has entrusted to her.

1. What "dime-store" stuff are you holding on to?

2. What genuine treasure might God have for you?

3. Are you giving God your firstfruits (Proverbs 3:9)?

4. Are you saving and planning for your future? If yes, how? If no, why not?

5. Are you living within your means?

6. Are you able to eat at least one meal each day with your family gathered together at your table?

7. How would you define wealthy?

8. How valuable is time to you?

9. Do you spend your time and money investing in things of eternal value?

10. Do you have a budget? If yes, what benefits have you seen from having a budget? If no, how might a budget help you manage your money better?

11. Hebrews 13:5 says, "Keep your lives free from the love of money and be content with what you have, because God has said, 'Never will I leave you; never will I forsake you.'" Journal your thoughts about this verse here.

12. Are you putting your pursuit of material things ahead of your pursuit of God? Journal your thoughts here.

13. Write a description of a faithful steward.

14. Are you and your husband working together as a team in the area of finances?

15. Read Matthew 6:31–34. Journal your thoughts here.

WRITING YOUR LIFE PLAN
(Refer to chapter 9 in the *Living Life on Purpose* book.)

Pray

Take time now to journal specific prayers for yourself as a faithful steward. Remember to:

Acknowledge God as our provider, and adore Him for being our caretaker.

Confess your sins in this area and ask for forgiveness, remembering always that we must forgive others if we are to be forgiven.

Thank God. Write out prayers of thanksgiving. List things you are thankful for as a faithful steward.

Supplication. Ask God for whatever is on your heart. Pray for your specific needs in the areas of your time and money.

Here are some suggested scriptural prayers for yourself as a faithful steward:

- That God be the master I serve, not money. That I always remember that God knows what I need and will provide for my family and me (Matthew 6:24, 32–33).

- That I be content in any situation, whether with plenty or in want. That I know the secret to my happiness is not found in money but in God and the fact that He will never leave or forsake me (Philippians 4:12–13; 1 Timothy 6:6; Hebrews 13:5).

- That I know only God is able to fill my heart with joy. If I faithfully love and serve God with all my heart and soul, He will faithfully provide for me (Deuteronomy 11:13–15; Psalm 4:7; Proverbs 28:20).

- That the true treasures of my heart not be the temporary things of this world but rather heavenly treasures that are eternally significant. That I would be wise in discerning the difference (Proverbs 15:16; Matthew 6:19–21).

- That I will always be a cheerful giver and willing to share generously with others. That I always remember that it is more blessed to give than to receive (Acts 20:35; 2 Corinthians 9:7; 1 Timothy 6:17–18).

_____

_____

_____

_____

_____

_____

_____

_____

_____

_____

_____

_____

Understand God's Word

Journal what God's Word says about your purpose as a faithful steward. Review Scriptures we've studied as well as any others you wish to include here.

_____

_____

_____

_____

_____

_____

_____

_____

_____

Now for a biblical portrait of a woman who knew her purpose as a faithful steward, let's dig a little deeper into God's Word and study our friend, the Proverbs 31 woman.

O the beloved Proverbs 31 woman. "A wife of noble character who can find?" (v. 10a). I think that to myself every day. I love a greeting card that portrays a frazzled woman on the front cover. When you open the card, it says, "Where are those servant girls when you need them?" Ha ha!

In considering being a faithful steward, we must think about the fact that we are the vessels God is entrusting with time and His money. That puts being a faithful steward into perspective, doesn't it?

Let's take a look at the time and money aspect of the Proverbs 31 woman. First we find the mention of her being valuable: "She is worth far more than rubies" (v. 10b).

There is a great value placed on you. You are to be such a good steward that your husband places his full confidence in you. If it is your duty to keep up with the car payments, mortgage, and other bills, a trust has been given to you. If you are the one buying the groceries, clothes, and other necessities, your husband needs to know that you are spending the family's money wisely.

QUESTIONS

1. "She brings him good, not harm, all the days of her life" (v. 12). What area of your life do you need to be more trustworthy in? Is it finances? Is it time?

2. Let's read further on the Proverbs 31 woman. "She selects wool and flax and works with eager hands. . . . She considers a field and buys it; out of her earnings she plants a vineyard" (vv. 13, 16). Is that you? Are you making wise purchases for your family? Are you spending money where it needs to be spent? Are you investing money and time where God wants it invested? What commitment can you make to God today in these areas?

3. "She opens her arms to the poor and extends her hands to the needy" (v. 20). Is that you? Is your home run so smoothly that you are available to others in their time of need? Are you available to cook a meal or clean a house for a person in need? What commitment can you make to God today in the area of giving some of your time and money to those in need?

4. "When it snows, she has no fear for her household; for all of them are clothed in scarlet" (v. 21). Is your home prepared for the unexpected? What commitment can you make to God today in the area of preparedness?

5. "She watches over the affairs of her household and does not eat the bread of idleness" (v. 27). Is that you? Are you watching over your time and money? Are you teaching your children God's principles for time and money management? What commitment can you make to God in glorifying Him with all that He's entrusted to you?

6. Why are you entrusted with so much? Because you are a daughter of the King whom He loves mightily! Please don't be overwhelmed, but rather be overjoyed that the Father loves you so much. He is patient and will help you in the areas where you fall short. Remember His words of encouragement to you: "Many women do noble things, but you surpass them all" (Proverbs 31:29). Journal your thoughts here.

_____

_____

_____

_____

_____

_____

_____

_____

Record Key Scriptures

Journal Scriptures here where God has revealed a spiritual truth to you. Write the verse and what you feel God wants you to understand through His Word. Remember, each time you experience a spiritual marker in your role as a faithful steward, pull this section of your Life Plan out and write it down. If you run out of room in this journal, continue your writings

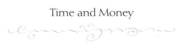

on separate paper and keep them in a special notebook.

_____

_____

_____

_____

_____

_____

_____

_____

_____

_____

Plan Your Goals

Write down goals for yourself as a faithful steward regarding both the time and money God has entrusted to you.

_____

_____

_____

_____

_____

Outline Your Action Steps

List your goals from above here, and under each one write out the necessary action steps needed to help you reach it.

Goal: _____

Action Steps: (1)_____ Deadline:_____

(2)_____ Deadline:_____

(3)_____ Deadline:_____

(4)_____ Deadline:_____

Goal: _____

Action Steps: (1)_____ Deadline:_____

(2)_____ Deadline:_____

(3)_____ Deadline:_____

(4)_____ Deadline:_____

Goal: _____

Action Steps: (1)_____ Deadline:_____
           (2)_____ Deadline:_____
           (3)_____ Deadline:_____
           (4)_____ Deadline:_____

Goal: _____

Action Steps: (1)_____ Deadline:_____
           (2)_____ Deadline:_____
           (3)_____ Deadline:_____
           (4)_____ Deadline:_____

Goal: _____

Action Steps: (1)_____ Deadline:_____
           (2)_____ Deadline:_____
           (3)_____ Deadline:_____
           (4)_____ Deadline:_____

Set a Realistic Schedule

Decide on a realistic deadline to accomplish each of your action steps. Make sure you schedule those steps above and on your calendar. If an action step is ongoing, write "daily" beside it and remember to schedule time for it each day.

Examine Your Progress

Write a plan to examine your progress here. If you plan to meet with an accountability partner or group, write out specific questions they should ask you. List areas in your role as a faithful steward they should ask you about and how they can pray for you. Specific questions and prayer requests:

_____

_____

_____

_____

_____

Here are some questions to consider from chapter 9 of *Living Life on Purpose:*

- Am I glorifying God in this area of my life?

- Am I working toward fulfilling my purpose in this area? How?

- How is my prayer life? Am I regularly praying for this area of my life?

- What have I recently learned from God's Word about this area of my life?

- What Scripture have I memorized to help me in this area?

- What action steps have I completed to help me move closer toward meeting some of my goals for this area?

- What goal or goals have I met?

- Am I managing my schedule well? Am I putting the "rocks" of my life first? Are there activities I need to eliminate from my schedule?

- Whom do I have to hold me accountable in this area of my life?

- Am I seeing positive life changes from having a Life Plan? If yes, list some of those here. If no, write out why not.

You will notice that there is enough room in your journal to examine your progress as a faithful steward once a month for one year.

JANUARY

_____
_____
_____
_____

FEBRUARY

_____
_____
_____
_____

MARCH

_____
_____
_____
_____

APRIL

_____
_____
_____
_____

MAY

_____
_____
_____
_____

JUNE

_____
_____
_____

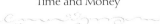

July

_____

_____

_____

_____

August

_____

_____

_____

_____

September

_____

_____

_____

_____

October

_____

_____

_____

_____

November

_____

_____

_____

_____

December

_____

_____

_____

_____

Part Fifteen

THE GIFT OF GODLY FRIENDSHIPS

(Refer to chapter 15 in the *Living Life on Purpose* book.)

PRINCIPLE # 6: The Proverbs 31 woman speaks with wisdom and faithful instruction as she mentors and supports other women and develops godly friendships.

1. Think about the word "friend." Does this word conjure up warm and wonderful thoughts and memories? If yes, journal your thoughts here.

2. Does this word sting because of past hurts and rejections? Journal your thoughts here.

3. Why do you think Jesus needed friends?

4. Examine the friendship circles model.

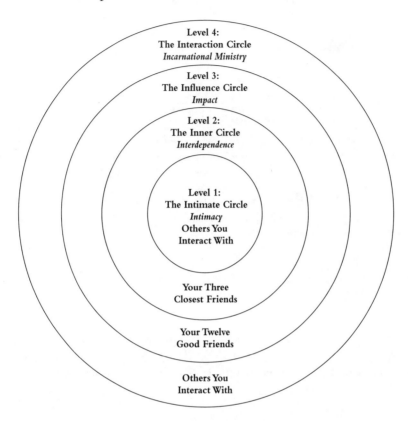

5. What word characterizes Level 1: "The Intimate Circle"?

6. Your relationship with God should be your most treasured friendship. How does God know that this is true in your life? What things do you do with God to build your relationship day by day? Journal your thoughts here.

7. What word characterizes Level 2: "The Inner Circle"?

8. Why must we choose the friends in this circle very carefully and prayerfully?

9. Jesus had three friends in this circle. These were the friends with whom He shared His deepest thoughts. Whom do you have in your Inner Circle?

10. Do these friends encourage you in your walk with the Lord? Do they themselves model godly character? Journal your thoughts here.

11. Do you need to ask God to send you some friends for your Inner Circle? Is there anyone who is currently in your Inner Circle who perhaps should not be? Journal your prayer here.

12. What word characterizes Level 3: "The Influence Circle"?

13. Jesus' other nine disciples fell into this category. These are the friends who are close enough to mutually influence and impact each other's lives. Whom do you have in your Influence Circle?

14. What must you remember when choosing these friends?

15. Do you need to ask God for some friends in this circle? Are there some friends in your Influence Circle who are not positive, godly influences on you? Journal your prayer here.

16. What word characterizes Level 4: "The Interaction Circle"?

17. These are the people with whom you have the opportunity to be a physical reminder of the characteristics of Jesus. Whom have you told about Jesus lately?

18. How can you seek to show the love of Christ to those you interact with?

19. Read and record Psalm 57:4.

20. Read and record Proverbs 25:15.

21. What are the ABC's of taming the tongue?

22. Which of these do you do well, and which do you need to work on?

23. What is your purpose as a godly friend? Journal your thoughts here.

Writing Your Life Plan

(Refer to chapter 9 in the *Living Life on Purpose* book.)

Pray

Take time now to journal specific prayers for yourself as a friend. Remember to:

Acknowledge God as the friend who sticks closer than a brother, and adore His loving-kindness.

Confess your sins in this area and ask for forgiveness, remembering always that we must forgive others if we are to be forgiven.

Thank God. Write out prayers of thanksgiving. List things you are thankful for as a friend.

Supplication. Ask God for whatever is on your heart. Pray for your specific needs as a friend. Also, write out specific prayers for your friends.

Here are some suggested scriptural prayers to pray for your friendships:

- That Jesus would be at the center of our friendships and that we would imitate God's love to one another. That the eyes of my unsaved friend would be open to the truth of the Gospel and that Jesus would become attractive to her because of the love she sees in me (Ephesians 5:1; 2 Peter 3:9).

- That our hearts would be tightly knit so that our friendship would not be broken. That we would be there to help one another when one falls. That we would be warm companions as this world can often be so cold (Ecclesiastes 4:10–12).

- That we would be faithful to pray for one another (James 5:16).

- That no unwholesome talk would come out of our mouths, but only what is helpful for building each other up so that it may benefit all who listen (Ephesians 4:29).

- That there would be no bitterness, anger, brawling, or slander between us. That we would be compassionate to one another, forgiving each other, just as Christ forgives us (Ephesians 4:31–32).

- Because we are holy and dearly loved children of God, let us always show one another love, compassion, kindness, humility, gentleness, and patience (Colossians 3:12–13; 1 John 4:7).

- That we would not just love with words but also with actions. That we would be willing to serve and help one another at all times (Proverbs 17:17; 1 John 3:18).

_____

_____

_____

_____

_____

_____

_____

_____

_____

_____

_____

_____

Understand God's Word

Journal what God's Word says about your purpose as a friend. Review Scriptures we've studied as well as any others you wish to include here.

_____

_____

_____

_____

_____

_____

_____

_____

_____

_____

_____

 Now for a biblical portrait of a woman who knew her purpose as a friend, let's dig a little deeper into God's Word and study Ruth and Naomi.

Friendships that God knits together with His holy hands are treasures. It amazes me how important friendships are, especially for women. You can become a part of someone's life and help lead her straight into God's will for her life. You have influence that could help steer her down roads leading to joy, peace, freedom, truth, and pure happiness. A story in the

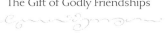

Bible that reminds me of such a friendship is that of Ruth and Naomi. After the death of her husband and sons, Naomi told her daughters-in-law that they should go back to their mothers' homes. "At this they wept again. Then Orpah kissed her mother-in-law good-by, but Ruth clung to her" (Ruth 1:14).

QUESTIONS

1. Have you ever run to the arms of a godly friend and clung to her? Explain.

2. Is there someone in your life who shows the love of Jesus to you? More important, is there someone in your life to whom you are showing the love of Jesus?

3. It is true that "a man reaps what he sows" (Galatians 6:7). The best way to have a friend is to be one. Can you think of someone who needs a godly friend right now? What special thing can you think to do for her?

4. Take time to write this on your calendar. Put a check mark here when you have scheduled this. ❏

5. Ruth told Naomi, "Don't urge me to leave you or to turn back from you. Where you will go I will go, and where you stay I will stay. Your people will be my people and your God my God" (Ruth 1:16). Godly friendships are the ones where Jesus is the Lord of the friendship. Read Ecclesiastes 4:9–12. Record any portion of that Scripture that you feel is especially important for friendships. Journal your thoughts about these Scriptures.

_____

_____

_____

_____

_____

_____

6. What friendships do you have where Jesus is the third cord?

7. What friendships do you have where the Lord is the lord of the relationship?

8. Are there any friendships you have that need to be given to the Lord today? Journal your prayer here.

9. Is there a broken friendship that you would like the Lord to heal?

10. Are you mentoring anyone in the Lord right now?

11. Are you being mentored in the Lord?

12. Ruth and Naomi's friendship led Ruth straight into the will of God. Ruth is in the royal family line of King David, which is the lineage of Jesus. Have you been used in a friendship to encourage someone toward the will of God?

13. John 15:13 says, "Greater love has no one than this, that he lay down his life for his friends." Are you that kind of friend? Write out a commitment to be the kind of friend God calls you to be.

Record Key Scriptures

Journal Scriptures here where God has revealed a spiritual truth to you. Write the verse and what you feel God wants you to understand through His Word. Remember, each time you experience a spiritual marker in your role as a friend, pull this section of your Life Plan out and write it down. If you run out of room in this journal, continue your writings on separate paper and keep them in a special notebook.

_____

_____

_____

_____

_____

_____

_____

_____

_____

_____

_____

_____

Plan Your Goals

Write down your goals for yourself as a friend.

_____

_____

_____

_____

Outline Your Action Steps

List your goals from above here, and under each one write out the necessary action steps needed to help you reach your goals.

Goal: _____

Action Steps: (1)_____ Deadline:_____

             (2)_____ Deadline:_____

             (3)_____ Deadline:_____

(4)_____ Deadline:_____

Goal: _____

Action Steps: (1)_____ Deadline:_____

(2)_____ Deadline:_____

(3)_____ Deadline:_____

(4)_____ Deadline:_____

Goal: _____

Action Steps: (1)_____ Deadline:_____

(2)_____ Deadline:_____

(3)_____ Deadline:_____

(4)_____ Deadline:_____

Goal: _____

Action Steps: (1)_____ Deadline:_____

(2)_____ Deadline:_____

(3)_____ Deadline:_____

(4)_____ Deadline:_____

Goal: _____

Action Steps: (1)_____ Deadline:_____

(2)_____ Deadline:_____

(3)_____ Deadline:_____

(4)_____ Deadline:_____

Set a Realistic Schedule

Decide on a realistic deadline to accomplish each of your action steps. Make sure you schedule those steps above and on your calendar. If an action step is ongoing, write "daily" beside it, and remember to schedule time for it each day.

Examine Your Progress

Write a plan here to examine your progress. If you plan to meet with an accountability partner or group, write out specific questions they should ask you. List areas in your friendships they should ask you about and how they can pray for you. Specific questions and prayer requests:

_____

_____

_____

_____

Here are some questions to consider from chapter 9 of *Living Life on Purpose:*

- Am I glorifying God in this area of my life?

- Am I working toward fulfilling my purpose in this area? How?

- How is my prayer life? Am I regularly praying for this area of my life?

- What have I recently learned from God's Word about this area of my life?

- What Scripture have I memorized to help me in this area?

- What action steps have I completed to help me move closer toward meeting some of my goals for this area?

- What goal or goals have I met?

- Am I managing my schedule well? Am I putting the "rocks" of my life first? Are there activities I need to eliminate from my schedule?

- Whom do I have to hold me accountable in this area of my life?

- Am I seeing positive life changes from having a Life Plan? If yes, list some of those here. If no, write out why not.

You will notice that there is enough room in your journal to examine your progress as a friend once a month for one year.

JANUARY

_____

_____

_____

_____

FEBRUARY

_____

_____

_____

_____

MARCH

_____

_____

_____

_____

APRIL

_____

_____

_____

_____

MAY

_____

_____

_____

_____

JUNE

_____

_____

_____

JULY

_____
_____
_____
_____

AUGUST

_____
_____
_____
_____

SEPTEMBER

_____
_____
_____
_____

OCTOBER

_____
_____
_____
_____

NOVEMBER

_____
_____
_____
_____

DECEMBER

_____
_____
_____

Part Sixteen

REACHING OUT

(Refer to chapter 16 in the *Living Life on Purpose* book.)

PRINCIPLE # 7: The Proverbs 31 woman shares the love of Christ by extending her hand to help with the needs in the community.

1. Read Matthew 11:28–30. Journal your thoughts about these verses.

2. The prophet Isaiah wrote, "Everyone who is called by my name, whom I created for my glory, whom I formed and made" (43:7). According to this verse, what is your ultimate purpose?

3. Have you ever tried to carry a yoke put on you by anyone but God? Journal your thoughts here.

4. What torch are you to carry in this race of life?

5. What do you need to do to be a qualified torchbearer? Journal your thoughts here.

6. Have you been in the shadow of the cross?

7. Have you felt the touch of the nail-pierced hands?

8. Has His crimson blood washed clean your sin-stained life?

9. It's time to carry the torch. Are you willing?

10. What battles will you face because you are touching others for Christ?

11. How can you dress yourself for battle? List your spiritual armor and what each piece protects.

12. How did the story about the wives of Weinsberg touch your heart? Journal your thoughts here.

13. Are you willing to fulfill your purpose as a servant? Journal a prayer to God here.

WRITING YOUR LIFE PLAN

(Refer to chapter 9 in the *Living Life on Purpose* book.)

Pray

Take time now to journal specific prayers for yourself as a servant of God. Remember to:

Acknowledge God as the ultimate model of a servant, and adore His sacrificial love.

Confess your sins in this area and ask for forgiveness, remembering always that we must forgive others if we are to be forgiven.

Thank God. Write out prayers of thanksgiving. List things you are thankful for as a servant of God.

Supplication. Ask God for whatever is on your heart. Pray for your specific needs as a servant. Also, write out specific prayers for those you are touching through your church and in the community.

Here are some suggested scriptural prayers to pray for yourself as a servant:
- That I offer my body as a living sacrifice, holy and pleasing to the Lord. That I never lack zeal but keep my spiritual fervor in serving, following, and holding fast to the Lord (Romans 12:1, 11; Deuteronomy 13:4).
- That I never judge or condemn others. That I am quick to forgive and quick to give. For as I give, it will be given to me (Luke 6:37–38).
- That whatever I do, I work at it with all my heart because it is the Lord I am serving, not men (Colossians 3:23).

Here are some suggested scriptural prayers for those you serve:
- That the eyes of their hearts may be enlightened so that the Lord would be their light and their salvation (Psalm 27:1; Ephesians 1:18).
- That the Lord would hear the cry of the afflicted and encourage them (Psalm 10:17).
- That they would not be afraid, suffer shame, be disgraced, or humiliated. That they may be able to say with confidence that the Lord is their helper (Isaiah 54:4; Hebrews 13:6).

- That they would know that there is no condemnation for those who are in Christ Jesus. That they would know that Jesus did not come to condemn them, so neither should anyone else condemn them (Romans 8:1).
- That they would give praises of joy to God for all He has done for them. That they would trust in His holy name (Psalm 33:21; 118:15).

_____

_____

_____

_____

_____

_____

_____

_____

_____

_____

_____

Understand God's Word

Journal what God's Word says about your purpose as a servant of God. Review Scriptures we've studied as well as any others you wish to include here.

_____

_____

_____

_____

_____

_____

_____

_____

_____

_____

_____

Now for a biblical portrait of a woman who knew her purpose as a servant, let's dig a little deeper into God's Word and study Rahab.

We meet Rahab in Joshua 2. Moses had just died, and Joshua was God's chosen replacement for Moses. He was commanded by God to get ready to cross the Jordan River into the land He had promised the Israelites. Joshua sent two spies ahead of the children of Israel to go look over the land of Jericho they were approaching. The king of Jericho was told of the spies and heard that they had come to Rahab the prostitute's house for help. Rahab had hidden them. She believed in them.

QUESTIONS

1. Have you ever changed someone's life by believing in her?

2. Who has the Lord placed on your heart to help, encourage, and mentor in God's love?

3. Rahab hid the two spies on the roof under stalks of flax. She told the king that they had left when it was "time to close the city gate." She told the spies before they lay down for the night, "I know that the Lord has given this land to you and that a great fear of you has fallen on us, so that all who live in this country are melting in fear because of you. We have heard how the Lord dried up the water of the Red Sea for you when you came out of Egypt, and what you did to Sihon and Og, the two kings of Amorites east of the Jordan, whom you completely destroyed. When we heard it, our hearts melted and everyone's courage failed because of you, for the Lord your God is God in heaven above and on earth below" (Joshua 2:8–11). When was the last time your "heart melted" in awe of the Lord our God?

4. Rahab caught glimpses of the Almighty through the stories circulating the town about the amazing things He had done. As a result she decided to believe that He was truly the God of heaven and earth, and her faith was born. God is still in the miracle business. Record a time from your life where you witnessed one of God's miracles.

5. Rahab welcomed the opportunity to serve God because of her faith. The Bible tells us that whatever we do for each other in the name of Jesus, we are to consider to have done for Jesus Himself. What have you done in Jesus' name lately?

6. Rahab asked the two spies to show kindness toward her and her family by sparing their lives. The two spies replied, "Our lives for your lives" (Joshua 2:14). In John 15:13, Jesus says, "Greater love has no one than this, that he lay down his life for his friends." We are called by God to love each other deeply (1 Peter 4:8) and to love our neighbors as ourselves (Matthew 19:19). Are you loving that way?

7. God is looking for servants to further His kingdom and to love and care for His children. Are you the kind of person God can count on? Are you willing to make that commitment to God? All He requires is a heart devoted to Him. He does all the rest. You will be amazed by how God will use you. You may be the next Esther, Rebekah, Hannah, Ruth, Naomi, or Rahab. Only God knows what your honored call is. But, remember two things: one, there is an honored call for your life and two, it all starts and ends with your heart. Please don't ever catch yourself feeling that God could never use you. Remember, God used Rahab despite her sin. He revealed Himself to her and she left her life of sin and shame. Is there some sin or shame in your life that you need to leave behind? Journal your thoughts here.

8. We have all sinned and fallen short of God's glory. Satan would love nothing more than to condemn us and render us ineffective for God's kingdom. Romans 8:1–2 says, "Therefore, there is now no condemnation for those who are in Christ Jesus, because through Christ Jesus the law of the Spirit of life set me free from the law of sin and death." Is there anything you feel condemned for?

9. Read John 8:31. What must you do to be a disciple of Jesus?

10. In "Part 1: Your Foundation," we looked at John 8:32: "Then you will know the truth, and the truth will set you free." Once you "abide in God's Word" (see John 15:1–8), then you will know the truth. Who is the truth?

11. What does Jesus promise to do for you?

12. Rahab did not question God's ability to use her, save her, and adopt her into His chosen people. Read Joshua 6:25.

13. Now turn to Matthew 1:5, and read an amazing detail of Rahab's life. Whose lineage is Rahab a vital part of?

14. John 8:36 says, "So if the Son sets you free, you will be free indeed." Do you have any doubt that God could use you? Do you have any doubt about your freedom in Christ?

15. You see, my friend, if Jesus sets you free, you are free indeed. You've been set free from secrets, shame, and condemnation. Do as Rahab did, turn from any sin that seeks to entangle you, and live as one of God's very own. Let God heal you and use you to touch others with His grace, mercy, forgiveness, and love. Who needs you to share the love of Christ by extending your hand to her?

Record Key Scriptures

Journal Scriptures here where God has revealed a spiritual truth to you. Write the verse and what you feel God wants you to understand through His Word. Remember, each time you experience a spiritual marker in your role as a servant of God, pull this section of your Life Plan out and write it down. If you run out of room in this journal, continue your writings on separate paper and keep them in a special notebook.

_____

_____

_____

_____

_____

_____

_____

_____

_____

_____

_____

Plan Your Goals

Write down your goals for yourself as a servant of God.

_____

_____

_____

_____

_____

Outline Your Action Steps

List your goals from above here, and under each one write out the necessary action steps needed to help you reach your goals.

Goal: _____

Action Steps: (1)_____ Deadline:_____

(2)_____ Deadline:_____

(3)_____ Deadline:_____

(4)_____ Deadline:_____

Goal: _____
Action Steps: (1)_____ Deadline:_____
           (2)_____ Deadline:_____
           (3)_____ Deadline:_____
           (4)_____ Deadline:_____

Goal: _____
Action Steps: (1)_____ Deadline:_____
           (2)_____ Deadline:_____
           (3)_____ Deadline:_____
           (4)_____ Deadline:_____

Goal: _____
Action Steps: (1)_____ Deadline:_____
           (2)_____ Deadline:_____
           (3)_____ Deadline:_____
           (4)_____ Deadline:_____

Goal: _____
Action Steps: (1)_____ Deadline:_____
           (2)_____ Deadline:_____
           (3)_____ Deadline:_____
           (4)_____ Deadline:_____

Set a Realistic Schedule

Decide on a realistic deadline to accomplish each of your action steps. Make sure you schedule those steps above and on your calendar. If an action step is ongoing, write "daily" beside it, and remember to schedule time for it each day.

Examine Your Progress

Write a plan here to examine your progress. If you plan to meet with an accountability partner or group, write out specific questions they should ask you. List areas in your role as a servant they should ask you about and how they can pray for you. Specific questions and prayer requests:

_____
_____
_____
_____
_____

Here are some questions to consider from chapter 9 of *Living Life on Purpose:*

- Am I glorifying God in this area of my life?

- Am I working toward fulfilling my purpose in this area? How?

- How is my prayer life? Am I regularly praying for this area of my life?

- What have I recently learned from God's Word about this area of my life?

- What Scripture have I memorized to help me in this area?

- What action steps have I completed to help me move closer toward meeting some of my goals for this area?

- What goal or goals have I met?

- Am I managing my schedule well? Am I putting the "rocks" of my life first? Are there activities I need to eliminate from my schedule?

- Who do I have to hold me accountable in this area of my life?

- Am I seeing positive life changes from having a Life Plan? If yes, list some of those here. If no, write out why not.

You will notice that there is enough room in your journal to examine your progress as a servant once a month for one year.

JANUARY

_____

_____

_____

_____

FEBRUARY

_____

_____

_____

_____

MARCH

_____

_____

_____

_____

APRIL

_____

_____

_____

_____

MAY

_____

_____

_____

_____

JUNE

_____

_____

_____

JULY

_____

_____

_____

_____

AUGUST

_____

_____

_____

_____

SEPTEMBER

_____

_____

_____

_____

OCTOBER

_____

_____

_____

_____

NOVEMBER

_____

_____

_____

_____

DECEMBER

_____

_____

_____

Part Seventeen

LET GOD DO AMAZING THINGS WITH YOUR LIFE

Take time now to write out a letter of commitment to let God do amazing things with your life. As you write this letter, incorporate things that you have learned throughout this study. Be sure to include ways your heart has been encouraged, your mind challenged, and your walk with the Lord strengthened.

_____

_____

_____

_____

_____

_____

_____

_____

_____

_____

_____

_____

_____

_____

_____

_____